The Opening of
the Suez Canal

From November 16 to 21, 1869, amid great pageantry, and surrounded by heads of state, celebrities, artists, and journalists, Khedive Ismail of Egypt and Vicomte Ferdinand Marie de Lesseps of France officially opened the first modern water route across the Isthmus of Suez. Before the canal was built under the direction of de Lesseps, sea trade going from Europe to the Orient had sailed around Africa's Cape of Good Hope and then eastward across the Indian Ocean. The Suez Canal, which dramatically shortened the distance between East and West, was a commercial success almost from the day it opened, but it was also the focus of international rivalries between France and England, England and Egypt, and in our own time between Egypt and Israel. In 1956, the Egyptian government nationalized the canal. Eleven years later, when the Israelis seized the east bank of the canal, the Egyptians responded by shutting the waterway to all traffic. While an agreement was sought, the old sea route around Africa to the East was revived, and long oil pipelines and giant transport planes also carried some of the goods that normally would have gone by way of the Suez Canal, the water gateway between East and West.

PRINCIPALS

THE FRENCH

Emperor Napoleon I of France who, as a general in the French army in 1798–99, directed a study examining the feasibility of building a canal linking the Mediterranean and Red seas.

Barthélemy Prosper Enfantin, a visionary who dreamt of the marriage between East and West, supervised an early study (1847) on construction of a canal.

Linant de Bellefonds, also called *Linant Bey,* a French engineer employed by the Egyptian government who made invaluable canal studies and assisted in building the canal.

Vicomte Ferdinand Marie de Lesseps, the diplomat who first conceived of the canal while in quarantine in 1832 and succeeded in directing the financing and building of the canal betwen 1854 and 1869.

Emperor Napoleon III, ruler of France while the canal was being built and whose wife, Empress Eugénie, was a cousin and loyal supporter of de Lesseps.

THE BRITISH

Henry John Temple, Viscount Palmerston, prime minister of Great Britain during most of the period when the canal was being built and an outspoken opponent of the idea.

Lord Stratford de Redcliffe, British ambassador to Turkey 1851–57, who also worked to prevent the building of the canal.

Benjamin Disraeli, first Earl of Beaconsfield, prime minister who purchased Khedive Ismail's shares in the canal company in 1875.

THE EGYPTIANS

Mehemet Ali, pasha of Egypt 1805–48, an opponent of the idea of building a canal across the Isthmus of Suez.

Abbas I, pasha 1848–54, another opponent of the canal.

Said Pasha, 1854–63, friend of de Lesseps during whose reign actual work on canal began.

Ismail Pasha (later khedive), 1863–79, who continued Said's support of de Lesseps but whose extravangances led him into bankruptcy and caused him to sell his shares in the canal company to Disraeli.

In 1869 the royal steam yacht l'Aigle, belonging to Empress Eugénie of France, led an escort fleet through the Suez Canal, marking the formal opening of the canal.

THE OPENING OF THE SUEZ CANAL

NOVEMBER, 1869
A Water Gateway Joins
East and West

Carol Zeman Rothkopf

A World Focus Book

FRANKLIN WATTS, INC.
NEW YORK | 1973

Maps by George Buctel

Photographs courtesy of:
Charles Phelps Cushing: pp. iv, 26; French Embassy
Press and Information Division: pp. 18, 52; Library of
Congress: pp. x, 9, 23, 31, 34; The New York Public
Library Picture Collection: pp. 7, 12, 17, 28, 41, 45, 46,
49, 54, 58, 61, 63, 64; United Nations: pp. 71, 72, 75

Library of Congress Cataloging in Publication Data

Rothkopf, Carol Zeman.
    The Opening of the Suez Canal.

    (A World focus book)
    SUMMARY: A history of the Suez Canal—its
building, opening, and operation.
    Bibliography: p.
    1. Suez Canal—Juvenile literature. [1. Suez Canal]
I. Title.
DT154.S9R68   962'.15'04   72-6893
ISBN 0-531-02166-1

Contents

For Paul,
Who Helped Me to Dig

The Opening of
the Suez Canal

COSSON. SMEETON

Excited crowds watch the opening ceremonies of the canal.

"The Greatest Drama"

Allah! Bestow thy Benediction upon Europe who, as Thou seest, has come among us today. Bestow thy benediction upon the enterprise which promises to enrich our poor nation. Bestow thy benediction upon our master and father Ismail, who has presided over these great labors. Bestow thy benediction upon all peoples. And we prostrate ourselves at thy feet, O Allah!

With these words, the sheik Ibrahim el Sakka of El Azhar offered the first of three blessings that began the ceremonies opening the Suez Canal on Novmber 16, 1869. The poor nation of which Sheik Ibrahim spoke was Egypt. Its master and father was the khedive Ismail who served as the viceroy of the sultan of Turkey, the overlord and real ruler of Egypt. On that hopeful day, however, more than a century ago it seemed quite possible that the canal might restore to Egypt the independence, power, and fame that it had lost nearly three thousand years earlier.

Now that men had succeeded in carving a waterway across the Isthmus of Suez linking the Mediterranean and Red seas, wealth would surely come to Egypt. Honor would be bestowed on every man associated with its creation. Most of the thousands of people crowded into the Mediterranean Port Said on that November day would have agreed with the journalist Henry Stanley, who called the opening of the canal the "greatest drama ever witnessed or enacted in Egypt."

The drama of the opening continued with the blessing of the canal by Roman Catholic and Greek Orthodox priests. The

1

double blessing was said to symbolize the unity of mankind that the canal would provide by linking together East and West.

Following the blessings, a sermon was read by Monseigneur Bauer, confessor to the empress Eugénie of France, the guest of honor at the opening. The monseigneur said that men would henceforth divide history into two parts — before and after the creation of the canal. Bauer ranked Ferdinand de Lesseps, the Frenchman who directed the building of the canal, with Christopher Columbus, and ended his sermon by appealing to the Almighty to

> *Make of this river not only a passage to universal prosperity, but make it also a royal road of peace and of justice; of the light, and of eternal truth. O God, may this highway bring men together, but above all may it bring them to Thyself; and may it be to everyone propitious, for time and for eternity.*

Although the monseigneur's words may seem a trifle too high-flown and hopeful for what was, after all, only a waterway across the desert, they accurately reflected the feelings of a good number of people at the time. Notable among them was de Lesseps himself, who had conquered every kind of obstacle from conniving diplomats to immovable rocks to bring into being his dream of a canal across Suez.

In November 1869, de Lesseps could look with justifiable pride at the canal that would not have been built without his stubborn determination. And it was easy for him and for every thinking person to imagine the benefits the canal would bring to Europe and Asia, the Americas and Africa.

2

Where once ships had had to take the tedious route around Africa to reach the Orient, now the journey would be shortened by some 4,000 miles — a tremendous saving in time and expense. It followed that the internationally owned and directed canal would bring the people of the world closer together — a noble goal summed up in the Latin motto de Lesseps chose for the canal: *Aperire terram gentibus* — "to open the earth to all mankind."

In sum, there seemed every reason to celebrate the canal's opening in a spectacular way. In addition, for Khedive Ismail the opening of the canal presented a unique and splendid opportunity to demonstrate to the world in general and to the sultan of Turkey in particular what an enlightened, generous, and independent ruler he was.

The date for the opening festivities was selected in 1867, long before some of the most serious obstacles to the actual navigation of the waterway had been removed. In July 1869, with some of the same obstacles still solidly in place, the khedive set out for Europe. His intention was to invite as many of the crowned heads of state to his party as he could conveniently and elegantly house in one of his eight palaces. He made the trip without advising the Turkish sultan of his intentions and even more seriously without considering how unwilling most European governments would be to offend the Turkish government. The sultan and his ministers were well aware of the khedive's plots, but did not interfere.

As it turned out, there was not much reason for the sultan to fret about the khedive's mission. European royalty understood the balance-of-power principle too well to risk offending Turkey

MEDITERRANEAN SEA

Damietta

Port Said

Rosetta Branch

NILE DELTA

Damietta Branch

Lake Manzala

Bay of Pelusium

Pelusiac Branch

Suez Canal

El Qantara

ISTHMUS OF SUEZ

Lake Ballah

Necho's Canal

Zagazig

Bubastis

Ptolemy's Canal

Wadi

Tumilat

Fresh Water Canal

Ismailia

Jisr Ridge

Lake Timsah

Pharoahs' Canal

Serapeum Ridge

N

Nile River

Nile River

Nile River

Suez Water Canal

Great Bitter Lake

Little Bitter Lake

★ CAIRO

Shallufa Ridge

Necho's Canal

Suez Canal

E G Y P T

Suez

SINAI

GULF OF SUEZ

SUEZ CANAL

0   10   20   30   40
Miles

Nile River

Ferdinand de Lesseps

for the sake of little Egypt. The only reigning monarchs to accept the khedive's hospitality were Empress Eugénie of France and Emperor Franz Josef of Austria-Hungary.

Eugénie agreed to come because she was de Lesseps's cousin and because she and her husband, the emperor Napoleon III, had supported the canal project when few others did. According to contemporary gossip, Franz Josef agreed to come only when he learned that the king of Prussia was sending his son the crown prince as his delegate. Since Franz Josef's delegate would have been a mere archduke, Austria would have been outranked at the opening ceremonies and that would have been intolerable to the Austrian national honor.

The kings of Sweden, Norway, and Greece declined their invitations. The king of the Netherlands delegated his brother, Prince Henry, to go; Russia and Great Britain agreed to send their ambassadors to the sultan's court at Constantinople — General Ignatiev and Mr. Henry Elliot respectively — as their representatives.

In addition to these distinguished guests, another thousand people representing the professions and the arts were invited to attend the opening ceremonies, with all their expenses paid by the khedive. Of this thousand, a more select group of one hundred was invited to come to Egypt a month ahead of schedule to tour the landmarks of the ancient land — again as guests of Ismail. Among this select group were such well-known persons as the Norwegian playwright Henrik Ibsen; the French writers Émile Zola, Théophile Gautier, and Alexandre Dumas; the English founder of international tourism, Thomas Cook; and a group of less familiar but then equally important people.

Curiously, considering how many professional artists were

present, the fullest accounts of the opening celebration found their way into newspapers and magazines, not into books. Photography was, of couse, still very primitive, so these accounts were decorated with rather romantic and very charming pen and ink drawings, or water colors. Judging from these sources the average European tourist expected Egypt in November to be miserably tropical and dressed accordingly. Sun hats, veils, turbans, and an exotic assortment of tinted glasses to protect against the sun and the eye diseases for which Egypt was known, were considered essential parts of the appropriate costume. In fact, the temperature was much more moderate.

Before the select group of one hundred had time to weary of Cairo, the pyramids, and other equally colorful attractions, it was time for the real festivities to begin at Port Said. Port Said had not existed until 1859 and it still had the raw look of a new city in 1869 when the eyes of the world turned to it. But even that rawness had a certain charm in the light of the dazzling fireworks display on the night of November 16. Ships flying the flags of all nations were docked in the magnificent harbor. The quays of Port Said were crowded with invited and uninvited quests. Some were dressed in the ornate and stately style of mid-nineteenth-century Europe. Others, from more remote corners of the earth, wore turbans, burnooses, caftans, and veils. The poorest of the uninvited spectators — drawn to what they knew to be an historic occasion — literally carried their households on their backs and slept wherever they could find a little space. The honored guests rested more snugly aboard their yachts or in hotels.

At eight o'clock sharp on the morning of November 17, the hush of excited waiting ended in a burst of whistles, sirens, and cheers as the yacht *l'Aigle,* with Empress Eugénie and Ferdi-

The first guests — elegantly attired — are greeted warmly as they arrive in Alexandria for the inauguration of the canal.

nand de Lesseps aboard, entered the Suez Canal. Bands alongside the embankment played military tunes as one after the other of the fleet of about seventy ships followed *l'Aigle* into the canal at ten to fifteen minute intervals.

Faithfully following the rules of protocol the next ships to enter the canal were those of Emperor Franz Josef. His ships were followed by the gunboats of the crown prince of Prussia. Then came the prince and princess of Holland, General Ignatiev of Russia, and then — far down the line — his excellency, the British ambassador, aboard the yacht *Psyche*. The snub to Britain, even in the detail of her late entry into the canal, was totally deliberate, for no other major power had provided such concerted and tireless opposition to the building of the canal.

The procession of ships entering the canal continued until nightfall. Meanwhile at Ismailia, the new city on Lake Timsah about halfway through the canal, the khedive and thousands of other people lined the banks to catch the first glimpse of *l'Aigle* as it steamed into the harbor. When the empress's ship appeared late in the afternoon the khedive went aboard to welcome Eugénie and to congratulate de Lesseps once again on his achievement. The greatest part of the festivities now began.

Ismail had transformed the city that was named for him into a fabulous setting for his enormous party. There, in the midst of the sand, he had erected a palace, elaborate buildings, triumphal arches, flower-garlanded streets, and even soup kitchens for those thousands of uninvited guests who might not otherwise have eaten. Elaborate banquets were served to the invited that evening at the palace and in vast canopied dining areas. According to one estimate eight thousand people enjoyed the khedive's hospitality on the night of the seventeenth alone. And the party

8

Port Said, a new city still rough around the edges, is bathed in fireworks, music, and pageantry.

was far from over when the last plates were cleared away. Dancers, jugglers, singers, and fireworks provided entertainment far into the night, while in the Arab encampments nearby the melancholy music of the desert dwellers could be heard until dawn.

Thursday, November 18, was clear and sunny, an ideal day for the picnic that had been planned — a picnic at which Empress Eugénie astonished and alarmed a number of people by insisting on riding a camel. She even rode camelback to the next stage of entertainment that afternoon — a diversion provided by Arab horsemen, magicians, jugglers, sword swallowers, and musicians.

In the evening a grandiose party for some four thousand guests was held in the khedive's palace. The palace, which was less than a year old, was ornately decorated with crystal chandeliers, huge mirrors, gilt chairs, marble-topped tables, and priceless rugs. One sharp-eyed visitor noticed that the mirrors were so newly hung that they had not yet been cleaned and the manufacturer's labels were still in place. To serve the guests in all this splendor were a thousand waiters in scarlet uniforms and powdered wigs.

Franz Josef, a thoughtful husband, wrote his wife long letters every day while he traveled, and this stupendous party, which he attended with the fashionplate Empress Eugénie on his arm, was dutifully reported to the absent Elizabeth in Vienna. To reassure Elizabeth's always prominent feelings of jealousy, Franz Josef wrote that Eugénie had grown quite plump and had lost much of her former good looks. (Henrik Ibsen, however, thought Eugénie was "as beautiful as Cleopatra.") As for the khedive's party, Franz Josef wrote "There was only one thought in all our minds . . . how to get out . . . and the Empress and I did all we

10

could to hurry up the supper. We were bound to wait for it, as the most magnificent preparations had been made, and the menu consisted of more than thirty dishes." It was long past midnight when the weary guests were able to leave.

The next morning, November 19, *l'Aigle* and fifteen other ships began the journey to Suez. They passed the night at the Bitter Lakes with a more muted exchange of visits and still another fireworks display.

On the morning of November 20, *l'Aigle* entered the Red Sea near the port of Suez as the guns on the embankment fired a twenty-one-gun salute and the troops shouted to Empress Eugénie, "God protect you! God protect you!" As one after another of the ships completed the 100-mile trip through the canal after about sixteen hours of actual traveling time, the British Admiral Milne cabled London a simple message: "Empress, *Psyche* . . . arrived. Canal is a great success."

For de Lesseps this understated praise from the British was perhaps the greatest of all triumphs. Later, on a visit to England, Queen Victoria honored de Lesseps with the Grand Cross of the Star of India. Emperor Napoleon offered de Lesseps the title duke of Suez, but he declined. It was as de Lesseps that he had struggled to cut a water highway through the desert and it was as de Lesseps that he had triumphed where so many before him had failed.

UEZ CANAL.

N. Y. PUBLIC
PICTURE COL

When the canal linking the East and the West was completed, it was the realization of a dream that reàched far back into history.

Builders and Dreamers

Ferdinand de Lesseps's achievement in opening the modern Suez Canal was based on his remarkably full and accurate knowledge of the dreamers and builders who had blazed the trail across the isthmus for him. Although de Lesseps's achievement was unique, the idea for it was almost as old as civilization itself.

A canal joining the Nile River and Red Sea may have been built as early as the reign of the Egyptian Pharaoh Sesostris I who died in 1926 B.C. At least that was the belief of such ancient historians as Aristotle, Strabo, and Pliny. An inscription on the Great Temple of Amon at Karnak in central Egypt suggests that such a canal was still in use during the reign of Seti I who died in 1290 B.C.

The canal of the pharaohs followed a somewhat different route than the modern one. Ships from the Mediterranean sailed down the eastern branch of the Nile to Bubastis (near modern Zagazig) north of Cairo. From there a canal cut across the Wadi Tumilat to the Bitter Lakes. Wadi is the name given to a stream bed or valley in the dry regions of Africa so it is clear that the pharaohs' canal followed natural routes wherever possible. At that time the Bitter Lakes still drained directly into the Gulf of Suez in the Red Sea, so the last part of the journey, like the first, followed an existing water route.

The drifting sands slowly closed the outlet of the Bitter Lakes and a barrier grew up that finally shut down the pharaohs' canal. Near the end of the sixth century B.C., Pharaoh Necho II decided to cut a new channel from the Bitter Lakes to the Gulf of Suez. In the fifth century B.C., Greek historian Herodotus re-

13

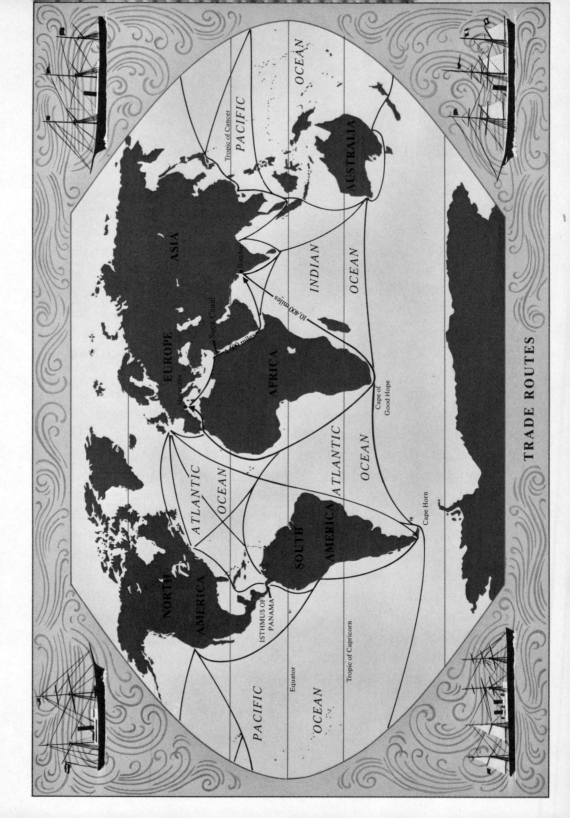

TRADE ROUTES

corded a full and eerily prophetic account of Necho's problems as a canal builder:

> It was Necho who began the construction of the canal to the . . . gulf, a work afterwards completed by Darius the Persian [reigned 522–485 B.C.]. The length of the canal is four days journey by boat, and its breadth sufficient to allow two triremes [an ancient galley having three banks of oars] to be rowed abreast. The water is supplied from the Nile. . . . The shortest distance from the Mediterranean, or Northern Sea, to the Southern Sea, or Indian Ocean . . . is just a thousand stades, or about 125 miles. This is the most direct route — by the canal, which does not keep at all a straight course, the journey is much longer. The construction of the canal in the time of King Necho cost the lives of 120,000 Egyptians. Necho did not complete the work, but broke it off in deference to an oracle, which warned him that his labor was all for the advantage of the 'barbarian' — as the Egyptians call anyone who does not speak their language.

Whether one believes in oracles or not, the history of the canals across Suez from that time to our own has shown that its strategic importance has made the waterway a tempting prize for whoever was the reigning "barbarian" of the hour. It is said that Necho did not remain discouraged for long, for he is known to have sent an expedition around Africa to India. Because the journey took the Egyptian fleet about three years, it did little to help their transportation problems.

As Herodotus explained, Necho's canal failure became the triumph of the Persian monarch Darius the Great who briefly dominated the Middle East. Not surprisingly it was the Romans,

when they in turn dominated the known world, who made the.
next important repairs and improvements on the old canal of the
pharaohs. The Roman emperor Trajan (A.D. 98–117) is credited
with having built a new stretch of canal from the Mediterranean
to Bubastis because by his time the eastern branch of the Nile
had grown too shallow for ships to use.

Until the fall of Rome in the fifth century A.D., the canal
was a busy route. Merchants from distant Arabia, India, China,
and islands of the southeast Pacific sent their rarest merchandise
— wild animals, spices, fine fabrics, and exotic jewels — to Rome
by way of the canal. But when Rome fell the peoples of Europe
became disunited again. War replaced peace and the wealth of
the imperial state became the poverty of disunity. No one needed
the magnificent merchandise that came by way of the canal
and the passage grew silent again.

It was not until the seventh century A.D. that dreamers again
began to see how desirable — and perhaps how dangerous — a
link between East and West by way of the canal could be. From
Baghdad, where the wise caliph Harun al-Rashid (764?–809)
ruled, diplomats traveled westward as far as the court of Charle-
magne and eastward to pay tribute to the T'ang emperors in
China. It was only natural that such an internationally minded
ruler as Harun should think of reopening the canal across Suez.
It was no less natural that his advisers should have pointed out to
him how vulnerable their frontiers would be to enemy attacks if
the canal were reopened. Harun al-Rashid forgot about the canal
and so, it seemed, did everyone else.

The tireless "ships of the desert," as camels are called, made
up the endless — and expensive — caravans that replaced the
sailing ships on the canal as a way of transporting goods across

16

Before the canal was built, camels were the "ships of the desert."

Egypt. Even this route lost some of its importance when Marco Polo opened the overland route to China in the thirteenth century. The opening of the sea route around Africa to the Orient by the Portuguese at the end of the fifteenth century made the trip by camel caravan even less important to traders. The sea route was, of course, far longer than the camel or canal route across the isthmus, but it was infinitely safer as no enemies lay in wait in pirate ships or robbers' ambushes. It was also much less expensive to send goods in a relatively large ship over the whole distance from Europe to Asia than to load and unload the merchandise — first on a ship, then on a camel, and then on a ship again. The long route around Africa was satisfactory to the most powerful merchant nations of Europe. Great Britain, in fact, still favored it over the canal literally up to the entrance of the *l'Aigle* into the channel at Port Said on November 17, 1869. As one observer said, the overland route across Suez was open to "vexations, interruptions, tolls, extortions, and insults." The route around Africa, on the other hand, was "comprehensive, safe, bold, truly English."

Thus it remained for a less powerful but equally ambitious seafaring nation to open the water route across Suez again. In the summer of 1798, the French general Napoleon Bonaparte conquered and occupied Egypt in an attempt to cut off England from its territories in India. The French government also recognized the moment as ideal for developing its own route to the markets of the Orient. Napoleon was ordered with remarkable straightforwardness to arrange for the opening of a canal across Suez.

Napoleon I, who, after conducting a land survey, saw the promise in building a canal.

As a result, Napoleon and a group of officers, engineers, and scholars left Cairo on Christmas Eve 1798 and began a survey of the overland route of Muslim pilgrims to the holy places in Arabia and of traders and empire builders with dealings in the East. Napoleon found traces of the old canals of the pharaohs and in the waters off the run-down and filthy little town of Suez he recognized a potentially fine harbor. It was on his orders that the harbor at Suez was deepened and that a naval shipyard was established there on the banks of the Red Sea. The precise engineering plans for the canal itself were to be drawn up more cautiously and thoughtfully by Napoleon's chief engineer, Jean-Baptiste Lepère.

Lepère's final report recommended building a canal quite similar to that of the ancient pharaohs. He argued that a direct canal from the Mediterranean to the Red Sea could not be built because, since the Red Sea at high tide was over 30 feet higher than the Mediterranean at low tide, there would be floods in the Nile Delta area. Lepère's conclusion violated the observable physical truth but at the time of this report, only a few very clear-headed mathematicians troubled to argue with his assertion.

It appeared again that a direct canal across Suez was to remain a dream forever. And for the moment it did not seem to matter much. In 1801 the English had driven the French army out of Egypt and resecured their route to India and the Far East. The hardiest travelers and the most urgent mail made their way across the overland route. Everyone and everything else that had to make the trip did so by way of the Cape of Good Hope. Clearly the next wave of dreamers and builders who considered linking the Mediterranean and Red seas would have to combat not only natural forces like wind, sand, and stone, but also the more subtle ambitions of nations vying to control a highly strategic area. The "barbarian" of whom the oracle warned Necho was still an ominous presence in Egypt in 1832, the year de Lesseps came to Alexandria as a member of the French Foreign Service.

Enter de Lesseps

De Lesseps came to Egypt in 1832 as a diplomat because a career in the French diplomatic service had been traditional for de Lesseps men since the mid-eighteenth century. As loyal servants of various French governments, the de Lesseps had acquired many honors. One of Ferdinand's uncles had been made a noble by King Louis XVI; his father, Mathieu, had been made a count by Napoleon I. Through his Spanish-born mother, Ferdinand was a cousin of Eugénie Montijo who was to become the empress Eugénie of France in 1853 when she married Napoleon III. In other words, the fates had provided Ferdinand de Lesseps with an invaluable background and allies for the vast task he confronted in winning support for building the Suez Canal.

But in 1832 when de Lesseps sailed for Egypt nothing could have been further from his mind than canal building. At the age of twenty-six, being posted as France's vice-consul to Cairo was an exciting opportunity for a young man who had so far served only in Lisbon, Portugal, with his uncle, and in Tunis with his father.

On the ship de Lesseps took to Egypt from Tunis one of the passengers suddenly died of an unknown disease. It was feared that the cause of the man's death was cholera, which was as contagious as it was dangerous. To make sure the contagion would not spread, all the ship's passengers were held in quarantine when they arrived in Egypt. The French consul-general thoughtfully brought de Lesseps a number of books to read to

Ferdinand de Lesseps was the individual most responsible for building the Suez Canal.

keep him from growing bored during his detention. Among the books was Lepère's report on "The Canal of the Two Seas." Thus the consul-general must be credited with one of the most important loans in history, for with this one report he helped to change the geography of the world.

It is certain that de Lesseps's imagination was captured by what Lepère had written, but when he assumed his consular duties he was much too busy to study canal-building. Along with the ordinary daily chores of a consular office, came the opportunity to make new friends and to discover a strange and historic country. In addition, there was an extraordinary demand on de Lesseps's genuine skill of helping others. During one of the feared and always tragedy-filled cholera epidemics that were so common at that time, de Lesseps won the affection of the Egyptians and high honor from his own government for his part in easing the suffering of the sick in Cairo and Alexandria.

Of course, for a well-placed young diplomat, life was not all work. Among the many friends de Lesseps made during his first stay in Egypt, some were to be of enormous importance to him in the future. One was a French engineer who worked for the Egyptian government. Linant de Bellefonds, or Linant Bey as he was called, was well-acquainted with the canal investigations and later was an invaluable aide to de Lesseps. Another good friend was the Dutch consul, S. W. Ruyssenaers, whose knowledge and understanding of Egyptian politics was to prove indispensable to de Lesseps.

At a still higher level of Egyptian society there was Mathieu de Lesseps's old friend from his days as consul in Egypt, the Pasha Mehemet Ali. Mehemet Ali had become the sultan of Turkey's viceroy, ruler, in Egypt in 1805 during the tumultuous days after the French army had been driven out of the country. A man of strong character but little education, the Albanian-born Mehemet Ali was as ambitious for himself as he was for Egypt. He strove to make the country as independent of Turkey as possible and tried to bring Egypt as much into the nineteenth century as he could, despite centuries of poverty and foreign rule. Its strategic location made Egypt a prize that the major European powers vied to control, but Mehemet Ali skillfully managed to retain control himself. His suspicion of foreigners did not include de Lesseps, whom he treated very warmly.

An even closer and ultimately more important friend of de Lesseps was the viceroy's youngest son, Prince Said — a boy of eleven when de Lesseps first met him. Said had the misfortune of being fat and lazy when his father would have preferred a thin and energetic offspring. Mehemet Ali devised a strict set of rules for his son that included such exercise as running around the city walls of Cairo and scampering up and down the masts of the ships that were anchored in the Nile. And, of course, he did not want Said to eat too much. De Lesseps was given the job of fencing and riding with the young prince, and the two became close friends. De Lesseps won Said's lifelong affection by treating him with respect when hardly anyone else did. Of at least equal importance was the fact that de Lesseps apparently could not resist the sad look on Said's face when he came to call and he would let the boy gorge himself on his favorite foods — spaghetti and French pastries — in the consulate kitchen.

Another remarkable person who crossed de Lesseps's path while he was in Egypt was Barthélemy Prosper Enfantin, the leader of a French philosophical group called the Saint-Simonians. The group took its name from the eighteenth-century Count Saint-

Simon, who had devised a form of communism that would abolish all property and divide society into castes ruled by an elect few. In the new state all the blessings of heaven would come to earth through the wise use of industry.

On another level entirely Enfantin saw himself as the founder of a new Christianity of which he represented one-half of Jesus Christ. The other, female, half had yet to be discovered. Enfantin saw himself and all Europe as the male element, which would be made whole through a symbolic marriage with his Oriental other half. Enfantin was so convinced of his role in the great scheme of things that he had his version of the society's bizarre costume of a loose tunic and tight trousers emblazoned across the chest with the words *Le Père*, the father.

In addition to his own marriage with the East, Enfantin visualized a geographic marriage of East and West through canals across Suez and Panama. After serving a prison term in France, Enfantin and his followers set out for the Middle East to launch the marriage of the continents. The sultan of Turkey was icily disinterested in Enfantin's ideas. The viceroy Mehemet Ali was ready to jail Enfantin for attempting to survey the Isthmus of Suez, which he feared was only the beginning of a French plot against Egypt. It is likely that it was only through de Lesseps's intercession that Enfantin was spared a term in an Egyptian jail and it takes little imagination to realize how personally fascinating the young de Lesseps must have found the colorful Enfantin and his canal-building ideas.

By the time de Lesseps returned to France in 1836 he had prepared a firm foundation for the future both through the

Mehemet Ali, viceroy of Egypt from 1805 to 1849.

Prosper Enfantin, the French philosopher who believed in a religious and geographical union of the East and the West.

friendships he had made and through the knowledge of Egypt he had gained. Suez was probably no more than an occasional thought, but he had learned through Lepère, Enfantin, and the growing use of the overland route across Egypt that a canal was not an unrealistic dream.

Once home in France, de Lesseps married Mademoiselle Agathe Delamalle and with her traveled to his next posts in Holland and Spain. By 1848 he had reached the rank of minister and was about to be transfered to a new post when revolution swept France. The Second Republic was established and Bona-parte's nephew, Louis-Napoleon, was elected prince-president. (By 1852 he had acquired enough power to change his title to emperor. The Second Republic became the Second Empire.)

France's short-lived Second Republic was only one of the changes that took place in 1848, a year of revolutionary upheaval in many parts of Europe. In Italy, which was still a collection of disunited states, the spirit of the times manifested itself in a new effort to drive out foreign rulers and establish a united na-tion. In the course of the upheavals the pope, fearing for his life, fled from Rome to Gaeta in the Kingdom of Naples. In Rome the short-lived Republic of Rome was founded under the leadership of the patriot Giuseppe Mazzini. Such important reforms as free elections, a free press, and government by laymen rather than clergymen were planned.

But the new French government, which had been elected by a large Catholic vote, felt threatened by Mazzini's actions and plans, and a detachment of French soldiers was dispatched to restore the pope to his city. De Lesseps was given the title of minister plenipotentiary and sent to Rome with the impossible task of finding a settlement that would satisfy both the pope and the Republicans. The only advice the French foreign minister gave de Lesseps was very vague. He said, "Your upright and enlightened judgment will inspire you according to circumstances." This was hardly helpful when de Lesseps confronted a pope who refused to promise reforms if he came back to Rome and a group of Republicans who refused to allow the pope back without a promise of reform and, furthermore, refused to allow the French army into their city.

De Lesseps worked hard to find a just solution but he was outmaneuvered by General Oudinot, who commanded the French forces and was eager for the glory of victory. Just as de Lesseps seemed to have achieved a settlement, Oudinot led his troops into Rome and simply announced the restoration of the pope. There was a tremendous outcry in France over the bungled mess, and de Lesseps was made the scapegoat of the affair. He was, in fact, the victim of his government's misjudgments and Oudinot's ambition.

At the age of forty-four de Lesseps resigned from the foreign service and retired to his family estate at La Chênaie (The Oak Grove) in Berry, in central France, to take up the life of a country gentleman. It was scarcely the existence one would have expected so ambitious, talented, and charming a man to have chosen, but it did provide — at last — time to think about and study the canal question.

Through his contacts in Egypt, de Lesseps learned that Linant Bey had surveyed the canal and found that it was a

Napoleon III, whose support helped de Lesseps win over other countries to his plan.

reasonable engineering project. From Enfantin, who had founded a society to study the possibility of building a Suez Canal, de Lesseps learned that Lepère's estimate of the difference in the level of the Mediterranean and Red seas was incorrect. Then, in 1852, de Lesseps prepared a memorandum of his own on building the canal and sent it to his Dutch friend Ruyssenaers in Cairo. Ruyssenaers advised de Lesseps that Mehemet Ali's successor, Abbas Pasha, who had become viceroy in 1848, was not likely to be interested in a foreign proposal for the canal because he was strongly anti-European and had only allowed the British to build the Alexandria–Cairo railway because he wanted them as allies against Turkey.

Within a year, de Lesseps's disappointment at this development was overwhelmed by a double tragedy in his own family. In the summer of 1853 his wife and one of his sons, Ferdinand, died of scarlet fever. All hope and all meaning seemed to have vanished from de Lesseps's life.

Concessions,
the Company...
and Complications

On September 15, 1854, de Lesseps wrote to his old friend Ruyssenaers in Cairo ". . . I was busy among masons and carpenters, putting an extra storey on [the] old manor-house, when the postman appeared in the courtyard with the Paris mail. The workmen passed my letters and papers from hand to hand. Imagine my astonishment when I read of the death of Abbas Pasha and the accession to power of that friend of our youth, the intelligent and warm-hearted Mohammed Said!"

At last, because two slaves had murdered Abbas Pasha, hope was reborn for de Lesseps. He immediately wrote Said to congratulate him and to say that he would like personally to pay his respects to him. Said replied promptly, inviting de Lesseps to come to Egypt at the beginning of November. In his letter to Ruyssenaers, de Lesseps exulted, "I want you to be one of the first to know that I shall punctually be there. What good fortune to find ourselves together again on our old ground in Egypt! Before I arrive, not a word to anyone about the project of cutting the Isthmus."

Said's welcome to de Lesseps was splendid. He was treated as a court favorite, given a palace in which to live, and invited to accompany Said on army maneuvers. The maneuvers provided de Lesseps with an almost ideal chance to put his ideas before the pasha without being overheard by all the ears in the gossiping court.

On the morning of November 15, de Lesseps awoke just as dawn was breaking. He stepped outside of his tent and saw a

perfect rainbow spread across the sky from west to east. It was an unmistakable sign to de Lesseps that the time had come to present his plan to Said. And so, almost fifteen years to the day before the canal was officially opened, de Lesseps described his plan for the canal to Said. When he was finished, the viceroy said simply: "I am persuaded. I accept your plan. We will concern ourselves during the rest of our expedition as to the ways of carrying it out. You may regard the matter as settled and trust to me."

It seemed as if the canal were as good as built. Unfortunately that was not the case. Historians agree that de Lesseps, in his single-minded and optimistic way, either scarcely imagined the difficulties that lay ahead, or simply did not allow himself to brood about them. After all he was almost totally unequipped for the job he had chosen. He was not an engineer and he had little business experience. What he did have was a vision and the intelligence, fortitude, and diplomatic skills to see him through. His belief in himself and his mission of uniting the world through the canal of the two seas made him as good as deaf to the unpleasant rumors that immediately began to circulate about him and his relationship with Said.

From the moment de Lesseps arrived in Egypt there were highly placed people who regarded him as a pirate, a swindler, and a crook interested only in enriching himself at the expense of Egypt. Nothing could have been farther from the truth because de Lesseps never saw the canal as a route to easy wealth for him-

Mohammed Said, who as a young boy was treated kindly by de Lesseps, backed his friend and became the most important national leader to support the project.

self, and in fact it never did bring him great financial reward. But at this stage of the proceedings no one knew much about de Lesseps except that he was a diplomat who had been involved in a diplomatic disaster.

De Lesseps's obstinate confidence in the future also made him somewhat blind to the shortcomings of his chief ally, Said. The fat little boy had grown into an immensely heavy man who was well educated, spoke excellent French, and had glorious ambitions for Egypt. But he was still childishly moody and moved easily from despair and rage to gaiety and expansiveness and back again into gloom. He eagerly started all kinds of worthwhile projects but backed down at the first sign of trouble. In short, he was not the most reliable ally one might have — but he was a powerful one and, after all, de Lesseps had little choice in the matter.

The stage for de Lesseps's difficulties was set at the special gathering of foreign consuls that Said called on December 1, 1854 to announce the canal agreement. The First Concession, as the agreement is known, had been worked out by de Lesseps and Said during their expedition with the army. According to the concession granted by Said, "Mons. Ferdinand de Lesseps shall form a company, the direction of which we confide to him, under the name of the Universal Suez Maritime Canal Company." It went on to state that the director of the company would always be appointed by the Egyptian government and that the term of the grant was to be ninety-nine years from the day the canal opened. The work on the canal itself was to be paid for by the company, but the Egyptian government would provide any state land and fortifications needed.

The concession allotted 15 percent of the net profits to be paid by the company annually to the Egyptian government; 75 percent to the company; and 10 percent to the founding members of the company. Article X of the twelve-point concession dealt with the reversion of the canal to Egypt at the end of the ninety-nine-year lease and was to be extremely important a century later. Article XII concluded ". . . we promise our true and hearty co-operation, and that of all the functionaries of Egypt in facilitating the execution and carrying out of the present powers." The vague wording of this article was to become a heavy burden for Egypt. Then, almost as an afterthought, at the very end of the concession was placed a most important reminder: "With regard to the works connected with the excavation of the Canal of Suez, they are not to be commenced until after they are authorized by the Sublime Porte."

The Sublime Porte, as the government of the Turkish sultan was known, was only one of the barriers that stood between de Lesseps and the swift realization of his dream. In the group of consuls gathered to hear Pasha Said announce the concession, the only one who was not immediately thunderstruck was Ruyssenaers. The French consul, M. Sabatier, hopefully anticipated an end to Britain's "petty opposition." Instead, the British consul, Mr. Bruce, heralded fifteen years of far from petty opposition, by remaining absolutely quiet while the other consuls politely applauded Said's announcement. Sabatier also incorrectly guessed his own government's reaction to the concession. At that very moment France energetically was trying to improve its troubled relationship with Britain. It was allied with England and Turkey against Russia in the Crimean War (1854–56) and was making every other effort to heal the wounds left over from Napoleonic times. It was not in France's interest at that moment to take part in any plan that was unacceptable to Britain.

The British themselves had a host of reasons for opposing the canal. The most important one was the simple but enormous fact that Britain did then truly rule the waves. As the world's leading sea power and with a vast overseas empire, anything that affected any part of its network was a major threat to the orderly progress of events. The British government remembered with perfect clarity that Napoleon I had invaded Egypt with the object of cutting Britain off from India. And here was another Frenchman, de Lesseps, apparently determined not only to build an unnecessary canal (Wasn't the sea route around Africa perfectly satisfactory?) but obviously about to turn Egypt and perhaps the whole Ottoman Turkish Empire into a French satellite. De Lesseps anticipated Britain's fears but hoped they would be overcome by what was to him the perfectly obvious fact that the canal would be a greater boon to Britain than to any other nation. He knew that he had no grand design for transforming the Mediterranean into a French lake, Egypt into a French colony, or the Middle East into a new French empire. His job was clear cut. He had to convince the Sublime Porte and the British government that all he simply wanted to build was a canal that would benefit all mankind.

De Lesseps began his long propaganda campaign in Constantinople where the British ambassador, Lord Stratford de Redcliffe, was awaiting him. A master diplomat, who was tremendously influential with the sultan and his advisers, Lord Stratford de Redcliffe seemed to many people to be virtually directing the affairs of the Ottoman Empire. The Turkish empire was known then as "the sick man of Europe" because it was so obviously near collapse and survived largely because it was in the interest of the great European powers to keep it alive as a buffer against Russian movement into the West.

When de Lesseps came to Constantinople in 1855, he did everything he could to persuade the British ambassador. He wrote to him, he pleaded with him at banquets, and finally he tried to slide around him to see the sultan, but it was useless. Clearly, if de Lesseps was to make any progress with the sultan, he would first have to change the mind of the British prime minister, Lord Palmerston.

De Lesseps prepared the way for himself in England with a barrage of letters to British political and business leaders, to newspapers, and to magazines — always explaining his simple, non-political plan for a canal across the Isthmus of Suez. Although popular opinion seemed to be on de Lesseps's side in England, the British government was not. Palmerston called de Lesseps a swindler in private and was only a little less rude in public. He and his associates found every reason to oppose the project, from purely political ones to technical objections, such as the idea that the canal would fill with sand as soon as it was dug.

Every day it became clearer that if the canal was ever to be built, de Lesseps somehow would have to by-pass the British and counteract their influence in Constantinople. This feat would require a larger propaganda program that would build up even greater popular support and win over to his cause both Napoleon III and the sultan.

For technical and propaganda purposes de Lesseps formed an International Scientific Commission in 1855 to survey the canal zone in detail and to prepare recommendations for the actual construction of the canal. De Lesseps, his old friend Linant Bey, four other Frenchmen, and a distinguished assortment of foreigners — four Englishmen, an Austrian, a Russian, an Italian, a Spaniard, a Dutchman, and a Prussian — took part in the survey. In 1856, the commission reported that the canal was a practical possibility and that the only unusual difficulties connected with it might be due to the necessity of building a port at the Mediterranean end.

Soon after the favorable engineering report appeared Said granted de Lesseps a Second Concession, which covered essentially the same ground as the first. The Second Concession did specify the exact route the canal was to follow and added the necessity of building a freshwater canal linking the Nile River and Suez Canal. In addition, it provided that four-fifths of the workmen employed on the canal had to be Egyptians. De Lesseps was designated as president of the canal company during the first ten years of its actual operation, and it was stressed that the canal "shall always remain open as a neutral passage." Then came the sticky concluding reminder that the sultan's approval had to be obtained.

The sultan's approval was still not forthcoming later in the same year when de Lesseps and Said reached a further agreement regarding the canal workers. It was agreed that the Egyptian government would provide as many workers as the company stated it needed and would provide their tools — picks, axes, and palm-leaf baskets — at cost to the company. The company was obliged to pay the workers at the rate of about 3 piastres (15

Lord Palmerston, then prime minister of England, opposed the canal.

cents) a day and to provide them with a piastre's worth of food; housing; and hospital care when needed, plus travel expenses to the work site.

All that remained to prepare the way for actual building to begin was the financing of the company, and, of course, the sultan's approval. De Lesseps discovered that it would be too expensive to have bankers sell shares in his company for him so he opened an office in Paris and became his own banker. A new barrage of propaganda was launched to arouse public interest in the sale of the shares. In a master stroke of diplomacy de Lesseps convinced Prince Jérôme Napoleon, the emperor's cousin, to act as a patron of the canal. This gave de Lesseps's endeavor a much-needed official air. When de Lesseps offered the shares for sale the French public was ready to buy.

Altogether 400,000 shares of stock at a price of five hundred francs (about one hundred dollars) per share, were offered. Since the company was meant to be international, only 220,000 shares were to be sold in France. The sales in France came to 207,111 shares, netting the company about $20 million, or about half the amount needed to build the canal according to the commission's estimate. But once again de Lesseps was too happy too soon.

The sales outside France did not begin to match de Lesseps's expectations. There were no buyers at all in England, the United States, Austria, or Russia. A handful of shares were purchased by investors in Switzerland, Italy, Spain, Holland, and Denmark. The internationally owned and operated canal was not going to be so international after all. In fact, after de Lesseps had convinced Ismail to buy all the outstanding shares of stock, as Said had once promised over-generously to do, the company became a Franco-Egyptian one just as Palmerston had feared.

In December 1858, de Lesseps incorporated the *Compagnie Universelle du Canal Maritime de Suez* — Universal Company of the Maritime Canal of Suez — although the shares were still not completely sold and there was now as obvious a shortage of funds as there was of political support for the task. The indomitable de Lesseps then wrote Said to request his permission to begin the actual work of digging the canal, arguing that the sultan's permission was needed only to operate the canal, not to build it. Said, who was feeling more and more oppressed by the forces arrayed against him on the canal issue, refused. De Lesseps decided to proceed on his intuitive understanding of Said's personality. Work began on the canal on April 25, 1859. He reasoned that if and when he needed Said's support he would be able to win it somehow.

Cutting the Canal

On April 25, 1859, Ferdinand de Lesseps, Linant Bey, and a small group of men stood on the spot where someday the waters of the Red Sea would enter the Mediterranean. An Egyptian flag was raised and the president of the Universal Company of the Maritime Canal of Suez delivered an inspirational speech. Then, one by one, de Lesseps and his companions moved some earth with a pickax to symbolize the beginning of the actual construction of the canal.

De Lesseps named the harbor city that would be built at the Mediterranean end of the canal Port Said in honor of the pasha, but neither the pasha nor any representatives of the interested governments was present at the ceremony. The first that Said and the consular corps in Cairo learned of de Lesseps's giant step was from the newspaper de Lesseps himself published about canal affairs.

An ordinary person can only marvel at de Lesseps's gamble. At this point he had the support of no government since Said was nervously trying to please the Turks, the English, and the French simultaneously; he did not have enough money and there was no certainty about raising more at that point; and in a short time even the members of his own company's administration in Paris would start asking, "What is de Lesseps up to?"

De Lesseps, with an unbelievable determination and a high degree of shrewdness, gambled on the things he knew best. He knew that the canal could be built and recognized that once it was, its merit would be proved to all the doubters who held back moral, political, and financial support. De Lesseps was also certain of his ability to win Said's support when that became neces-

Port Said in 1919. These reservoirs became the town's major source of water, replacing a freshwater canal and the old method of carrying casks across the desert by camels.

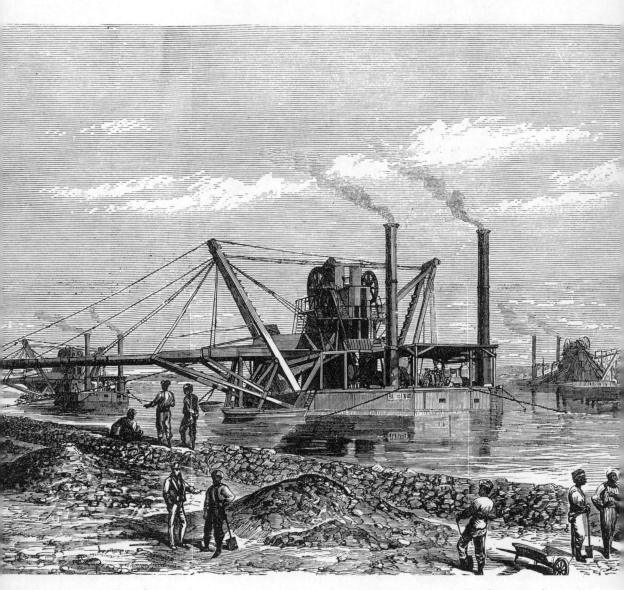

Work on the canal was done by steam-operated dredges and elevators.

sary. His hopes of getting Napoleon III's open endorsement also seemed to have improved. France, because of its share in victory in the Crimean War, and its conquering of the Austrian army in northern Italy in 1859, was no longer a defeated power trying to placate Britain. And, perhaps of equal importance, there were those more than 20,000 French shareholders. An unsatisfactory conclusion to de Lesseps's Suez adventure would be a major embarrassment to France, and that fact would help win Napoleon III to de Lesseps's cause.

Throughout the spring and summer of 1859 work on the canal proceeded slowly. De Lesseps was actively engaged in supervising the actual construction as well as reminding Said in quite blunt terms of his promises and obligations — and of the glory the canal would bring him. And, of course, he was working through various channels, including Empress Eugénie, to win Napoleon III's public support.

Finally, on October 23, 1859, de Lesseps met with the emperor. Napoleon asked de Lesseps why everyone seemed to be against the canal project. De Lesseps replied, "Sire, it is because everyone believes that Your Majesty does not wish to support us." Napoleon advised de Lesseps not to worry about that, saying, "You can count upon my support and protection." It was a most important victory for de Lesseps as it would serve to bolster the sagging faith of Said and others in the canal project. But there were still many other battles to be fought and literally thousands of problems, large and small, to be solved.

The actual job of building the canal proceeded in roughly three stages — the building of the harbor at Port Said, the creation of a canal that would supply fresh water to the Suez Canal Zone, and the cutting of the canal itself.

It turned out that the building of the harbor at Port Said would be one of the most difficult parts of the project. The future port was remote from sources of drinking water, food, and virtually every other necessity of life, but it was vital to have the port at which to unload machinery and supplies for the canal. The port grew rapidly despite the difficulties and by 1860 a visitor reported that a lighthouse, fourteen houses, a pier, jetties, and a breakwater were already built.

The freshwater canal, which ran from Zagazig to Lake Timsah (and later was extended north and south along the length of the canal) presented less difficult supply and engineering problems. Until the freshwater canal was built, casks of water were brought to supply depots on camel back and carefully guarded against theft. By the end of 1862 the first arm of the freshwater canal was completed. It followed the ancient traces of Necho's canal and involved the work of between 3,000 and 7,000 laborers. Working only with shovels and baskets into which the sand was dumped, the laborers had moved over 1 million cubic meters of soil.

At the end of 1862 another 15,000 to 20,000 workmen had completed digging the preliminary trace of the canal itself as far as Lake Timsah. To achieve even this partial step meant moving aside another 4 million cubic meters of sand and muck. The worst of this job was across the shallow Lake Menzaleh at the Mediterranean end of the canal where the workmen had to dig the muddy soil from the lake bottom with their bare hands. Using an ancient method, the workmen took the balls of mud they had dug up, squeezed them dry by pressing them against their chests, and then laid the lumps on the canal to bake completely dry. When one layer was dried by the sun, another layer was added,

*The freshwater canal running between Lake Timsah and Port
Said had been dug by thousands of hands.*

and so on. Then mechanical dredgers followed the workers' path, lifted the clay from the bottom of the lake, and added it to the mud banks. Eventually, strong 6-foot-high walls sturdy enough to carry men and supplies had been built on the canal banks.

Even as the work went forward there remained unsettling, unsolved problems. The money supply was far from sufficient for the task that still lay ahead; it was obvious that more machines would be needed to augment the work of the laborers; and finally, there were still tremendous diplomatic battles to win.

Since all the shares in the company had not been sold, and because the work was not going ahead as rapidly as had been expected, there was no hope of interesting other investors. De Lesseps's best hope for financial assistance was his old friend Said who, de Lesseps claimed, had promised to buy all the unsold shares in the company.

After Said's death in 1863 his nephew Ismail became pasha of Egypt. Although de Lesseps did not know Ismail as well as he had his predecessor, the two men came to recognize that they could be useful to each other. For de Lesseps, this meant that Ismail would honor Said's promise to support the canal with his power and as the purchaser of those unsold shares. Ismail's gradually growing support of the canal project was based on his belief that if he supported the French-run canal company he would gain the support of France itself in his long campaign to win greater freedom from the overlordship of the sultan. There is also the likelihood that he thought he might, somehow, be able to take over the canal company himself. Whatever the reasons that moved him, Ismail finally did buy the unsold shares, to de Lesseps's great relief, and spent a good portion of his fortune on the project.

50

Ismail, a man convinced that money could buy him anything, was almost simple-minded in his ignorance of the value of money. He used the vast resources of his treasury to bribe officials of the sultan to win him the loftier title of khedive; he embarked on a project to beautify and modernize Cairo; and he supported the canal. These projects and others moved Egypt into debt at the staggering rate of $40 million a year — a sum raised more and more often as the years went on by European bankers who charged astronomical interest rates. Of his total expenditure, about 20 percent went to the Suez Canal. Ismail fully earned having the town on Lake Timsah named for him.

But Ismail's reign did not start well for de Lesseps. The pasha's advisers and such familiar agents as the British ambassador and the powers at the Sublime Porte were urging Ismail to act against de Lesseps. And, at first, they succeeded.

In 1862 the British ambassador to the Porte, Sir Henry Bulwer, came to Egypt to see what progress had been made on the canal project. He was apparently more impressed than any previous British government figure because he advised London that the canal obviously was not quite the fantastically improbable undertaking that it had been thought. Bulwer even reported that it was quite likely that the canal could be completed. But he raised a new issue. "On general grounds of progress and humanity there are great objections as to the mode under which the French scheme is carried out." In plain words, Bulwer objected to the fact that forced labor was being used to build the canal, as, in fact, it had been on every Egyptian project since the dawn of time. However, in a decade that had witnessed the abolition of slavery in the United States and serfdom in Russia, the popular mood was rapidly turned against a French and there-

51

fore presumably enlightened company for using what amounted to slaves on a project that would benefit other Europeans. Before long the message reached the sultan and he ordered Ismail to stop all Egyptians from working on the canal.

It was a terrible blow to de Lesseps, but with his customary shrewdness he turned it to good advantage. As work dragged to a halt in the spring of 1864 it seemed to Ismail that the time had come to take over the project himself. But de Lesseps was not about to give up his or his shareholders' participation easily. Both sides finally agreed to let Napoleon III arbitrate the labor question and the matter of compensation that would be due the company from Egypt for withdrawing from the labor part of the concession agreement.

De Lesseps's luck held out. In August 1864 the emperor decided that the Egyptian government owed the canal company $16,800,000 to make up for withdrawing the labor force. It is not hard to detect Eugénie's hand in the decision that was so favorable to the company. More than ever she appeared as the kindest of all possible patronesses. The last human obstacle to the canal project vanished on March 19, 1866, when the sultan gave his long-hoped-for approval. Now nearly all de Lesseps's energy could be concentrated on the task of building.

With its new-found wealth from the Imperial Arbitration, as it was known, the company was able to bring engineers and machinery from France to Egypt that would make the work go far more quickly and easily. Dredgers, cranes, steam-driven excavators, and other contrivances worked rapidly, moving some 60

Empress Eugénie of France gave great emotional as well as financial support to de Lesseps.

53

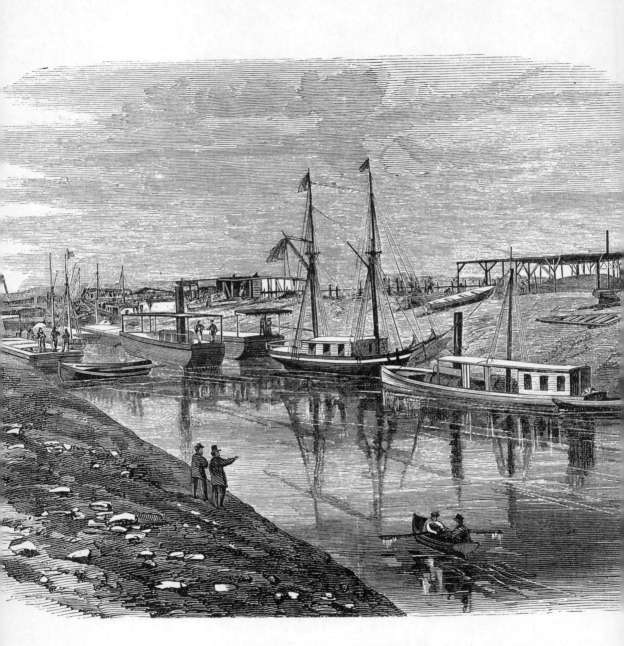

Some of the first ships to pass through the canal.

million cubic meters of earth between 1865 and 1869. (The workmen with their shovels and baskets had moved only about 15 million cubic meters in the six years between 1859 and 1865.) The towns of Port Said and Ismailia were completed and harbor facilities were installed at Port Said and Suez. The Sweet Water Canal was completed along the length of the canal. And even stubborn rock formations blocking the canal at Shallufa and Serapeum were removed.

One last and irritating obstacle appeared suddenly on the night before the canal was to be officially opened. An Egyptian ship, the *Latif,* ran aground while patrolling the canal to make sure the passage was clear for the next day's ceremony. Ismail personally rushed to the site near Qantara and helped supervise the refloating of the grounded ship. At eight o'clock the next morning Empress Eugénie and Ferdinand de Lesseps aboard *l'Aigle* led the procession into the canal.

For years to come the Suez Canal was to be considered one of the great engineering marvels of the ages. Two seas had been joined in a man-made, sea-level canal without locks that crossed 100 miles of once-barren desert. When it was opened the canal's surface width varied from 150 to 300 feet. Its depth was about 26 feet and its width at the bottom was 72 feet. Eight stations, like highway parking areas, made it possible for ships to pass each other without danger. Alongside the canal, the desert, newly fed by water, began to blossom. All this at a cost of almost $100 million — more than double the estimates the commission had made years earlier, but a small sum in terms of shortening the sea route to the Orient by over 4,000 miles.

Monarchs and ordinary men competed to find praise and medals enough for de Lesseps, whose vision, tenacity, skill, and tirelessness had been tested endlessly from the moment that he had first read about the canal of the two seas in 1832 to the glorious day in 1869 when the canal became a reality. De Lesseps had fulfilled his great dream of opening the world to all mankind. Unfortunately it was a dream that sometimes became a nightmare.

A Gift for the Queen

On November 25, 1869, at the age of sixty-four, the world-famous and still handsome and youthful widower Ferdinand de Lesseps privately celebrated the completion of the canal by getting remarried in a small chapel near Ismailia. His wife, Louise-Hélène Autard de Bragard, was the twenty-year-old daughter of an old family friend. The de Lesseps were to become the parents of twelve children, the youngest of whom was born when de Lesseps was eighty.

It would be pleasant to end the story of de Lesseps at this point in the loving circle of his large family but it was not to be so. The remaining years of his life were an extraordinary mixture of great acclaim for Suez and bitter tragedy arising from his efforts to build a canal across Panama.

Throughout the 1870s and part of the 1880s de Lesseps remained *le Grand Français* — the great Frenchman. He was a man who had brought honor to his own nation almost at the same time as its armies were being crushingly defeated at Sedan by the Prussians. The defeat led to the fall of the Second Empire and the flight into exile of Emperor Napoleon III and his wife Eugénie. De Lesseps remained in France, a living incarnation of the best of their reign. He was in demand everywhere as a consultant, a committee-member, and figurehead. Among his accomplishments during this period was service on the committee that raised the money for France's gift to the United States, the Statue of Liberty, and his presence at the actual dedication of the monument in New York Harbor. He easily could have won a seat in the National Assembly but declined. He was made a member of the very distinguished French Academy.

De Lesseps and his young wife with their large family, early in the 1890s.

In the midst of this shower of honors, however, there were still problems arising from his position at the head of the Suez Canal company. In its first complete year of operation — 1870 — only 486 transits were made through the canal representing a tonnage of 436,609. The riches the shareholders had expected to reap immediately from the opening of the canal were not forthcoming. Protest mounted again at the management of the company. Propaganda pamphlets appeared from the opposition with frightening titles like "The Agony of Suez . . . Its Approaching Ruin." Adjustments were made in the tolls charged for the use of the canal and gradually the shippers of the world switched to the new, shorter route to the East. By 1875 the shareholders in the company finally could begin to relax as the value of their shares began to rise along with the number of transits, which reached 1,494 in that year. (The figure was steadily to increase, except during the war years 1916–18 and 1940–43, to 21,250 transits of 274,250,000 tons in 1966.)

In other respects 1875 was a black year for the canal company and for its chief shareholder, the khedive Ismail. His reckless extravagance had led him and his country to the edge of financial disaster. Taxes of every kind burdened his people. Even the bankers who once eagerly loaned Ismail money now refused to do so. His last best hope was to sell his shares in the company.

Rumors that the khedive might be willing to sell his interest in the company had been in the air since 1870. By far the most interested possible purchaser was Britain, which earlier had scorned the project so totally. In fact, by 1875 almost four-fifths of the traffic through the canal was British. It was obvious even to the last defenders of the long British route around Africa that the nation's best interests in the East were better served by the shorter, more direct canal route.

When word reached British Prime Minister Benjamin Disraeli in November 1875 that the khedive was ready to sell and that no French group was ready to buy, he decided to act quickly. The story of Disraeli's purchase of the khedive's shares was as romanticized by him as any of the novels he had published, but beneath the fiction there was an essential truth. According to both the Disraeli version and to the observable facts, he learned of the khedive's offer to sell when Parliament was not in session to authorize the purchase, so money would have to be found somewhere else. Disraeli dispatched his secretary, Mr. Corry, to the banker Baron Lionel de Rothschild. Corry told Rothschild that Disraeli needed 4 million pounds sterling the next day. Rothschild, calmy peeling a muscatel grape, asked Corry, "What is your security?" Corry replied, "The British government." The baron replied, "You shall have it." At a commission of 2.5 percent, the Rothschild fortune stood to increase by another 100,000 pounds.

In his typically flamboyant way, Disraeli then presented the shares to Queen Victoria to whom he wrote:

It is just settled; you have it, Madam.
The French government has been out-generaled.

"The lifeline of the empire," as the canal came to be known, was now more British than ever before. Although it was not until

Prime Minister Benjamin Disraeli of Britain shrewdly tied his country's future to that of the canal when he bought Egypt's shares in the company.

60

1895 that the British gained the voting rights that went with the shares (because of complications arising from their ownership by the khedive), it was security enough for the moment to own 44 percent of the shares and to be a major user of the canal. The French power in the company and in Egypt was clearly no longer the threat feared by Palmerston and his generation of diplomats.

Meanwhile, in Egypt there were desperate, almost feverish attempts to stave off the next step — the complete collapse of Ismail's government and the occupation of Egypt by that most interested power — Britain. By 1879 the so-called Dual Control, by which Ismail had permitted representatives of France and Britain to more or less run his affairs, arranged for the sultan to depose Ismail. Ismail's son Tewfik, who had proved to be more loyal to the Anglo-French forces than to his father, became khedive.

But there were Egyptians who could not accept what amounted to a virtual takeover of their government by foreigners and awaited their opportunity to overthrow Tewfik and drive his associates back across the Mediterranean. In 1882 Ahmed Arabi, the minister of war, led a revolt against Tewfik and the Europeans. It was immediately seen as a threat against the khedive, the foreign interests in Egypt, and above all the security of the Suez Canal. De Lesseps — now a man of seventy-seven — appeared in Egypt in the midst of these troubles and struggled to remind the invading British forces of the canal's neutral status. He claimed, probably truthfully, that he had Arabi's word not to violate that status. But no one listened to the old man. In August of 1882 British troops occupied the canal company offices in Port Said and entered the canal, which was closed for five days. A month later, on September 13, 1882, the British forces routed

The canal company offices in Port Said. The take-over by British troops in 1882 marked Britain's control of the canal.

Arabi and the British occupation of Egypt had begun. It was to last until 1936, and British soldiers were to remain in the Canal Zone another twenty years after that.

The canal was now securely under British control, although still essentially under French direction. Improvements were made continually in the canal itself and traffic grew steadily. The route across the isthmus was beginning to function just as de Lesseps had imagined it would. Raw materials from the Orient were shipped via the canal to the industrialized nations of the West and then returned to the markets of the East, again by way of the canal. After a convention was signed by Great Britain, France, Germany, Austria-Hungary, Russia, Italy, Spain, the Netherlands, and Turkey in 1888, it even seemed that the canal's neutrality would be guaranteed in the future. The first article of the convention stated plainly that

> *The Suez Maritime Canal shall always be free and open, in time of war as in time of peace, to every vessel of commerce or of war, without distinction of flag.*
> *Consequently, the High Contracting Parties agree not in any way to interfere with the free use of the Canal, in time of war as in time of peace.*
> *The Canal shall never be subjected to the exercise of the right of blockade.*

It seemed that de Lesseps had been vindicated again. But his last project did not fare as well. In 1889, a year after the

The monument to "le grand français." Ironically, de Lesseps died in obscurity, his reputation in question, and years later, when his name was cleared and his honor restored, the statue was destroyed.

65

Suez Canal's neutrality had been firmly declared, de Lesseps's Panama Canal Company collapsed. In 1878, de Lesseps had become president of a French company formed to build a canal across the Isthmus of Panama. It had been a financial disaster that shook the young French Third Republic to its foundations. De Lesseps, who was brought to trial with his eldest son and partner, Charles, was sentenced to prison for his part in what was then thought to be a gigantic swindle of the kind Lord Palmerston had feared at Suez. In fact, it seems likely that de Lesseps was again made a scapegoat for his government as he had been in 1849. The sentence was not carried out, however, and de Lesseps spent his last years in retirement. He died, stripped of honor in his countrymen's eyes, on December 7, 1894. Three years later a larger-than-lifesize statue of him was erected at Suez. But even the statue was to prove as impermanent as the praise that had been lavished on the man himself.

The "Fortified Ditch"

By the time the last British troops were withdrawn from the Suez Canal Zone in May 1956 a great many changes had taken place in the canal itself and in the area around it. The canal had been enlarged several times to serve the ever-larger ships that carried cargo around the world. What is perhaps even more remarkable is that the canal had survived the bitter struggles of two world wars. Its neutral status had been preserved and, with the exception of a brief period during World War II, when bombing forced the canal's closing, it remained open throughout the conflicts.

As a result of World War II, Britain's role as an imperial power had been sharply reduced and its influence in distant lands was diminished as well. In 1952 the last of Mehemet Ali's descendants (a dynasty that was virtually established by the British), King Farouk, was overthrown and exiled from Egypt. The revolutionaries had been led by a group of army officers who, like Arabi before them, desired complete independence from foreign interference for Egypt. One of these officers, Colonel Gamal Abdel Nasser, became premier and the president of the newly established republic. Meanwhile, across the Sinai Peninsula a new nation, Israel, had come into being in 1948. From the day of its establishment Israel and Egypt were enemies. Egypt and the other Arab nations went to war to regain the Israeli territory for their own displaced Arab brethren in 1948 and 1949 but were driven back. All-out war was replaced by sporadic fighting and border raids until a United Nations Emergency Force was stationed on the Egyptian side of the border to enforce the armistice.

EUROPE and the MIDDLE EAST TODAY

Approximate extent of the Ottoman Empire 1832

N

UNION OF SOVIET SOCIALIST REPUBLICS

★ Teheran

IRAN

CASPIAN SEA

KUWAIT

★ Kiev

★ Riyadh

IRAQ

Baghdad ●

Euphrates R.

Tigris River

SAUDI ARABIA

SYRIA

Damascus ★

● Mecca

RED SEA

★ Ankara

TURKEY

Jerusalem
JORDAN
Aqaba
Gulf of Aqaba
Eilat
SINAI PEN.
Sharm el-Sheik

BLACK SEA

Beirut ●
LEBANON
ISRAEL
Gulf of Suez
Suez
Port Said

YEMEN

Sana ●

Gulf of

Istanbul
(Constantinople)

CYPRUS

Nile River

Aswan High Dam

★ Khartoum

Odessa ●

Lake Nasser

Alexandria ●
● Cairo

EGYPT

RUMANIA

Bucharest ★

R.

Danube

Sofia ★

BULGARIA

★ Athens

GREECE

CRETE

Benghazi ●

Belgrade ★

YUGOSLAVIA

ALBANIA

M E D I T E R R A N E A N   S E A

POLAND

★ Warsaw

Berlin ★
EAST
GERMANY

Bonn ●
WEST
GERMANY

CZECHOSLOVAKIA

Budapest ★

Vienna ★
AUSTRIA
HUNGARY

Venice ●

Bern ●
SWITZ.

I T A L Y

SICILY

Tripoli ●

LIBYA

NETH.

BEL.

Rome ★

Milan ●

TUNISIA

Tunis ★

UNITED KINGDOM

London ●

★ Paris

FRANCE

Marseilles ●

Algiers ★

ALGERIA

ATLANTIC

OCEAN

Barcelona ●

SPAIN

★ Madrid

Rabat ●

MOROCCO

PORTUGAL

Lisbon ★

Strait of
Gibraltar

It was against this troubled background that Nasser planned and worked to improve the economy of Egypt. One of his plans called for the building of a high dam at Aswan in Upper Egypt. It was estimated that the project, which would irrigate more land for farming and provide needed hydroelectric power for industry, would cost about a billion dollars. Egypt hoped to borrow this money from the United States, the Soviet Union, or perhaps even France or Britain. At one time the United States seemed about to underwrite the project but when Nasser demanded an answer to his request in July 1956. Secretary of State John Foster Dulles abruptly announced that the United States had decided not to take part in the project.

On July 26, 1956 — the fourth anniversary of the Egyptian revolution — an enraged Nasser gave a two-and-a-half-hour radio speech announcing that Egypt would immediately seize the canal and nationalize the company. "This Canal," he said, "is an Egyptian Canal. . . . In 1955 the income of the Suez Canal Company reached $100,000,000. . . . We . . . received only $3,000,000. . . ." His intentions were immediately clear. The revenues of the canal would pay for the building of the Aswan High Dam. And so, at the moment Nasser mentioned the code word "de Lesseps," men moved to seize the company offices in Cairo, Port Said, Ismailia, and Suez.

At one blow the international ownership and direction of the canal, the heart of de Lesseps's dream, vanished. The Suez Canal company had been disposed of. But the matter was far from settled. The French and British governments, with their historic interest in the canal, were infuriated by Nasser's action and profoundly worried by the prospect of his controlling the movement of ships through the canal and perhaps even closing it if it suited the needs of Egypt. Immense pressures were built up to persuade Egypt to return the canal to international control but they were resisted.

Then in November 1956 — in a move that is still wrapped in mystery and will be debated for years to come — Israel invaded and successfully occupied the Sinai Peninsula. British and French forces launched a land and air attack on Egypt and retook Port Said before the United Nations stopped the war from continuing. Nasser, now in the position of having had his country invaded, demanded that all foreign troops leave his country before he would reopen the canal, which the Egyptians themselves had blocked by sinking ships in it. On Christmas Day the last troops were gone, but on Christmas Eve, in one last violent gesture of protest against foreigners, a group of men had blown up de Lesseps's statue at Suez.

The canal was reopened in January 1957, and Nasser won the support of the United Nations for his contention that the canal was indeed Egypt's. As part of the price of regaining the canal into which Ismail had poured a fortune and for which thousands of lesser known Egyptians had given their lives, Egypt paid 28,300,000 Egyptian pounds to the shareholders in the Suez Canal Company. The last payment of this indemnity was paid in 1963, a year ahead of schedule. The Universal Suez Maritime Canal Company was reorganized as the Compagnie Financière de Suez, an investment company.

The Egyptians proved to be as competent as managers of the canal as their predecessors had been, and new improvements were made in the waterway immediately, while others were planned. One problem remained to threaten these designs for the future — the uneasy truce that still existed between Egypt and

70

The fighting in 1956 between Egypt and the new nation of Israel brought United Nations soldiers to the shores of the canal to help restore peace.

Workers clear the canal for its reopening in 1957; only ten years later, Nasser closed it again with a blockade against Israel.

Israel. Most observers agree that it was only the presence of the United Nations Emergency Force that prevented war in the years between 1956 and 1967. In view of this the world was very startled by Nasser's demand in May 1967 that the United Nations remove its force from his country. The secretary-general of the United Nations, U Thant, in an equally astonishing move, agreed to remove the troops, and the last of them departed on May 19, 1967.

Three days later Nasser announced a blockade of the Gulf of Aqaba and the Israeli port of Eilat — thus sealing Israel off from its exit to the Red Sea as he had earlier blockaded it from the canal. War was now almost inevitable and on June 5 the Israelis launched a lightning attack that succeeded in destroying three hundred Egyptian planes — three-quarters of its air force. In a few more swift strikes they took the Gaza Strip, Sharm el-Sheik, and the command of the two roads from the center of the Sinai Peninsula to the canal. Before the Six-Day War ended Israeli troops occupied the east bank of the Suez Canal.

At the end of the war the canal was filled with ships that had been trapped there by the outbreak of war. One by one they were permitted to leave the waterway but still the canal remained shut. The Israelis stated that they would not move back from the canal's east bank until their ships were permitted to use the canal. Egypt refused. The deadlock continued, deeply entwined with other disputes between the two countries. Time passed and sand began to drift into the canal. Egyptian soldiers stood poised on the west bank, Israeli troops guarded the east bank. All Lord Palmerston's darkest fears seemed to be coming true at once as the canal filled with sand and became a "fortified ditch."

The one-hundredth anniversary of the opening of the canal

passed in silence. The stalemate dragged on while the Soviet Union bolstered Egypt's defenses with new planes, missiles, and even pilots, according to some reports. The United States helped Israel to obtain new defense supplies as well. And all the while there were sporadic outbreaks of air and ground battles.

With the long closing of the canal came severe economic problems for Egypt and other nations as well. The canal had been most heavily used by tankers carrying oil to Europe and these, of course, now once more had to travel the long route around Africa. Prices of heating oil, fuel oil, and industrial oil rose. Other prices increased as well. The only groups that could really benefit from the closing were the major shipping companies in Norway and Greece which made more money by shipping goods the long way and oil-producing nations near Europe, like Libya and Algeria. Egypt itself lost the much-needed revenue from the canal, a sum that had reached $250 million in 1966, the last complete year of operation. A new refugee problem also had been created within Egypt, as the employees of the canal inhabiting towns all along the west bank had to find new homes and new jobs.

At first there were no great efforts to reopen the canal because both Britain and the United States feared that the chief beneficiary would be the Soviet Union, which needed the short cut to reach its expanding interests in the Indian Ocean and the Far East. But as the stalemate dragged on and prices rose as a result of the canal closing, new efforts were made to bring peace to the area. In the summer of 1970, Israel and Egypt accepted a

In modern times, barbed wire and fighter planes have replaced de Lesseps's vision of peace.

proposal made by United States Secretary of State William Rogers to accept a cease-fire throughout the Canal Zone. But the canal remained closed and no peace treaties were signed.

While the world watched and waited there were growing debates about the value of the canal itself to world trade. Was it not outmoded in an age of supertankers and giant jet aircraft? Could it possibly be renovated — if it were reopened — to serve the supertankers that were being built and planned? There seems to be general agreement that the canal could easily be expanded to handle the larger ships and that there was still a need for the sea route across the Isthmus of Suez. Obviously it is relatively simple to build a larger canal or tankers. It is incomparably more difficult to find a way of bringing peace to the Canal Zone so that de Lesseps's vision of a world open to all mankind can live again.

Chronology

609–593 B.C.	Reign of the pharaoh Necho who begins a canal from the Pelusiac branch of the Nile to the Red Sea.
285–246 B.C.	Reign of Ptolemy II who continues Necho's canal from Bitter Lakes to the Red Sea.
A.D. 98	Roman Emperor Trajan makes canal navigable again after years of disuse.
641–776	Muslims reopen Trajan's canal, but it is soon closed for strategic reasons.
1798–99	Engineers under command of General Napoleon Bonaparte examine possibility of building new canal linking Mediterranean and Red seas.
1805 (Nov. 19)	Ferdinand de Lesseps is born in Versailles, France.
1825	De Lesseps joins French foreign service.
1849	De Lesseps is sent as minister plenipotentiary to Roman Republic and as a result of mission resigns from French foreign service.
1850	Pasha Mehemet Ali of Egypt dies, succeeded by Abbas Pasha.
1854	Abbas Pasha dies, succeeded by Said Pasha, an old friend of de Lesseps. Said grants First Concession to build canal to de Lesseps.
1855	International Scientific Commission formed to examine possibility of building the canal.

1856	Commission gives favorable report on canal building, but opposition to idea grows rapidly in England and Turkey.
1858	De Lesseps, ignoring opposition, establishes Universal Company of the Maritime Canal of Suez.
1859	City of Port Said is founded on Mediterranean end of canal and work on canal itself begins.
1863	Said Pasha dies, succeeded by Ismail Pasha.
1864	International opposition to use of "forced labor" to build canal causes temporary cessation of work.
1866	Turkish sultan finally approves concession to build canal.
1869	Canal opens to traffic amid great festivities between November 16 and 21.
1875	Khedive Ismail sells his shares in Suez Canal company to Britain.
1879	De Lesseps becomes president of Panama Canal Company.
1882	As a result of war in Egypt, British occupy country.
1887–93	Panama Canal Company suffers financial failure, de Lesseps is tried and sentenced for his part in disaster, but sentence is never carried out.
1894	De Lesseps dies.
1936	Britain's occupation of Egypt ends but troops remain in Canal Zone.

1952	Egypt's King Farouk is overthrown by army officers.
1956	Colonel Gamal Abdel Nasser becomes head of Egyptian government. July 25 — seizes Suez Canal and nationalizes it. October — Israelis send troops toward Canal Zone. November 5 — French and British paratroops occupy Canal Zone.
1957	United Nations declares Suez Canal Egyptian and it is reopened to ships.
1963	All shareholders in Suez Canal company are repaid by Egyptian government.
1967	During Six-Day War, Israeli forces occupy east bank of canal, which is again closed to traffic.
1970	United States Secretary of State William Rogers proposes cease-fire in Canal Zone. Soviet Union moves missiles to area.
1972	Egyptians work on oil pipeline connecting ports on Red and Mediterranean Seas as a partial substitute for canal.
1972 to present	Efforts continue to find way of reopening canal and settling differences between Egypt and Israel.

Other Books to Read

Aubry, Octave. *Eugénie, Empress of the French.* Translated by F. M. Atkinson. Philadelphia: J. B. Lippincott, 1931.

Balfour, John Patrick Douglas (Lord Kinross). *Between Two Seas: The Creation of the Suez Canal.* New York: William Morrow & Company, 1968.

Beatty, Charles. *De Lesseps of Suez: The Man and His Times.* New York: Harper & Brothers, 1956.

Blake, Robert. *Disraeli.* New York: St. Martin's Press, 1967.

Burchell, S. C. *Building the Suez Canal.* New York: American Heritage, 1966.

Crawley, C. W. "The Mediterranean." *The New Cambridge Modern History.* The Zenith of European Power: 1830–1870, Vol. X. Edited by J. P. T. Bury. Cambridge: Cambridge University Press, 1960.

Farnie, D. A. *East and West of Suez: The Suez Canal in History, 1854–1956.* Oxford: Clarendon Press, 1969.

Grant, Neil. *Benjamin Disraeli: Prime Minister Extraordinary.* New York: Franklin Watts, 1969.

Herodotus. *The Histories.* Translated with an introduction by Aubrey de Sélincourt. Baltimore: Penguin Books, 1968.

Lesseps, F. de. *The History of the Suez Canal, A Personal Narrative.* Edinburgh: Blackwood, 1876.

————. *Recollections of Forty Years.* London: Blackwood, 1887.

Mansfield, Peter. *The British in Egypt.* New York: Holt, Rinehart and Winston, 1972.

Marlowe, John. *World Ditch: The Making of the Suez Canal.* New York: The Macmillan Company, 1964.

Morton, Frederic. *The Rothschilds*. New York: Atheneum, 1962.

Schonfield, Hugh J. *The Suez Canal in Peace and War: 1869–1969*. Rev. ed. Coral Gables, Florida: The University of Miami Press, 1969.

Smith, Dennis Mack. *The Making of Modern Italy*. New York: Harper Torchbooks, Harper & Row, 1968.

Thomas, Hugh. *Suez*. New York: Harper & Row, 1967.

Index

About the Author

Carol Zeman Rothkopf was born and educated in New York City. After receiving an M.A. from Columbia University she worked as an editor on a number of encyclopedias including *Our Wonderful World*, *The New Book of Knowledge*, and *Lands and Peoples*. She is the mother of three children — David, Paul, and Marissa — who have encouraged her to write books for them. Her favorite period in history is the nineteenth century, her favorite figures are the giants of that age, like de Lesseps, whose idealism, courage, and stubbornness helped them achieve their goals against almost overwhelming odds. Among her other books are *Tolstoy*, *Jean Henri Dunant*, and a number of First Books, including *Yugoslavia* and *East Europe*.

DATE DUE